Like our Facebook page
@RiddlesandGiggles

Follow us on Instagram
@RiddlesandGiggles_Official

Questions & Customer
hello@riddlesandgiggle

Easter Knock Knock Joke Book for Kids

by Riddles and Giggles™

www.riddlesandgiggles.com

FREE BONUS

Get your FREE book download

Easter Jokes & Would You Rather for Kids

- Contains a collection of Egg-cellent Easter Jokes and Would You Rather Easter-Themed Questions
- More endless giggles and entertainment for the whole family.

Claim your FREE book at www.riddlesandagiggles.com/easter

Or scan with your phone to get your free download

TABLE OF CONTENTS

WELCOME

Hi there, Jokester!

Knock-knock jokes are a great way for people to have fun and share laughs together.

Lots of people love to tell knock-knock jokes. Some are very funny. Some are just corny. Other knock-knock jokes make no sense at all. One thing we can agree on about knock-knock jokes is that kids love them!

I hope you are one of those kids because if you want a collection of funny, corny and laugh-out-loud knock-knock jokes, this book is for you!

The *Easter Knock-Knock Joke Book for Kids* is an awesome collection of good, clean fun knock-knock jokes that will make you roll your eyes, snort, giggle, groan and laugh out loud.

So, grab your Easter sweets and get ready for some funny and corny Easter knock-knock jokes!

You can enjoy reading the jokes on your own. You can also share the knock-knock jokes with everyone around you and take turns reading the jokes out loud.

PSST... you can also color in the Easter pictures and use this book as a coloring book AND a joke book!

TIPS ON HOW TO TELL A KNOCK-KNOCK JOKE

- Practice reading the joke out loud a few times to help you remember it. You may want to practice reading in front of a mirror.

- Find a family member or friend and ask them if they want to hear a knock-knock joke.

- As you tell the joke, remember to say it slowly and clearly so people understand every word.

- Adding a small pause helps to build up suspense and can make the joke even funnier.

- Deliver the final punch line. Remember to say it slowly, then wait for the laughs.

- If you mess up, that's ok. Move on and tell another joke. Remember, everyone loves knock-knock jokes!

1

EASTER EGG PUNS

Knock knock.
Who's there?
Dozen.
Dozen who?
Dozen anyone want Easter eggs?

Knock knock.
Who's there?
Eggstra.
Eggstra who?
E.T., the eggstra-terrestrial!

Knock knock.
Who's there?
Egg.
Egg who?
Egg-cellent joke, don't you think?

Knock knock.
Who's there?
Crack.
Crack who?
You crack me up!

KNOCK KNOCK JOKES FOR KIDS. EASTER EDITION

Knock knock.
Who's there?
Yolk.
Yolk who?
Like my Easter yolk?

Knock knock.
Who's there?
Egg-sactly.
Egg-sactly who?
Egg-sactly 50 eggs are
hidden for the
Easter egg hunt!

Knock knock.
Who's there?
Egg-stravagant.
Egg-stravagant who?
Don't the Easter
decorations
look egg-stravagant?

Knock knock.
Who's there?
Egg-citing.
Egg-citing who?
Isn't Easter an
egg-citing time?

Knock knock.
Who's there?
Egg-static.
Egg-static who?
I am egg-static about
eating my Easter eggs!

Knock knock.
Who's there?
Egg-splosive.
Egg-splosive who?
My tummy is feeling
egg-splosive from all
this Easter food!

Knock knock.
Who's there?
Egg-cercise.
Egg-cersise who?
We need to walk around the
block for some egg-cercise!

Knock knock.
Who's there?
Egg-ceptional.
Egg-ceptional who?
Doesn't all the Easter food
look egg-ceptional?

Knock knock.
Who's there?
Egg-streme.
Egg-streme who?
This Easter is going
to be egg-streme!

KNOCK KNOCK JOKES FOR KIDS. EASTER EDITION

Knock knock.
Who's there?
Egg-saggerate.
Egg-saggerate who?
Don't egg-saggerate about all your toys!

Knock knock.
Who's there?
Poaching.
Poaching who?
Stop poaching my
best yolks!

Knock knock.
Who's there?
Tegg-nology.
Tegg-nology who?
An iPad is my favorite
tegg-nology!

Knock knock.
Who's there?
Yolk.
Yolk who?
Don't yolk with me!

Knock knock.
Who's there?
Shell.
Shell who?
Let's shell-ebrate Easter!

Knock knock.
Who's there?
Omletting.
Omletting who?
Omletting this
joke slide!

EASTER EGG PUNS

Knock knock.
Who's there?
Rotten.
Rotten who?
Last one to the kitchen
is a rotten egg!

Knock knock.
Who's there?
Whisk.
Whisk who?
You might whisk getting sick
from too much chocolate!

Knock knock.
Who's there?
Egg-noring.
Egg-noring who?
Stop egg-noring me! Don't you
like my egg-cellent jokes?

Knock knock.
Who's there?
Cracked up.
Cracked up who?
This joke is not all it's
cracked up to be!

Knock knock.
Who's there?
Egg white.
Egg white who?
Egg white and the seven hens!

Knock knock.
Who's there?
Beaten.
Beaten who?
I got beaten in the
Easter egg hunt!

Knock knock.
Who's there?
Egg-scuse.
Egg-scuse who?
Egg-scuse me, please!

Knock knock.
Who's there?
Egg-spresso.
Egg-spresso who?
Mom likes a shot of
egg-spresso in the morning!

Knock knock.
Who's there?
Egg-sit.
Egg-sit who?
Please take the
next egg-sit out!

Knock knock.
Who's there?
Many.
Many who?
I have so many yolks, it
is not even bunny!

Knock knock.
Who's there?
Four.
Four who?
Four-eggs-ample!

Knock knock.
Who's there?
Yolks.
Yolks who?
Ha ha! This yolks on you!

Knock knock.
Who's there?
Negg-ative.
Negg-ative who?
Stop being so negg-ative!

Knock knock.
Who's there?
Egg-spert.
Egg-spert who?
I am an egg-spert at
telling Easter jokes!

Knock knock.
Who's there?
That's.
That's who?
That's all, yolks!

2

NAMES

Knock knock.
Who's there?
Howard.
Howard who?
Howard you like to go Easter egg hunting with me?

Knock knock.
Who's there?
Annie.
Annie who?
Annie body coming for Easter lunch?

Knock knock.
Who's there?
Howie.
Howie who?
Howie gonna find all
the Easter eggs?

Knock knock.
Who's there?
Chuck.
Chuck who?
Chuckolate is my
favorite kind of egg!

Knock knock.
Who's there?
Freddy.
Freddy who?
Are you Freddy for Easter?

Knock knock.
Who's there?
Tommy.
Tommy who?
I ate too many Easter
eggs, now my Tommy
is aching!

Knock knock.
Who's there?
Harry.
Harry who?
Harry up and help me
look for more
Easter eggs!

Knock knock.
Who's there?
Justin.
Justin who?
Justin the yard waiting
for the Easter egg
hunt to begin

Knock knock.
Who's there?
Noah.
Noah who?
Noah Easter bunny
or two?

Knock knock.
Who's there?
Luke.
Luke who?
Luke, it's the
Easter Bunny!

NAMES

Knock knock.
Who's there?
Hope.
Hope who?
Hope we get a lot of candy this Easter!

Knock knock.
Who's there?
Hayden.
Hayden who?
Hayden go seek
Easter eggs!

Knock knock.
Who's there?
Candice.
Candice who?
Candice Easter get
any better?

Knock knock.
Who's there?
Chase.
Chase who?
Chase Dad, he stole
your Easter basket!

Knock knock.
Who's there?
Eden.
Eden who?
Eden my Easter dinner,
I'll come out to play later!

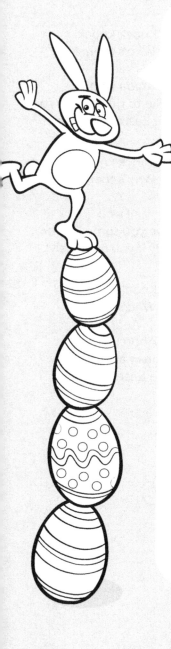

Knock knock.
Who's there?
Abby.
Abby who?
I am so Abby you are here for Easter!

Knock knock.
Who's there?
Anita.
Anita who?
Anita stop eating so
much Easter candy!

Knock knock.
Who's there?
Iva.
Iva who?
Iva craving for hot cross buns!

Knock knock.
Who's there?
Watson.
Watson who?
Watson the menu for Easter?

Knock knock.
Who's there?
Sadie.
Sadie who?
Sadie magic word and
I'll give you more
chocolate eggs!

Knock knock.
Who's there?
Ben.
Ben who?
Ben waiting for the
Easter Bunny!

Knock knock.
Who's there?
Aida.
Aida who?
Aida like to go hunting for
some Easter eggs now!

Knock knock.
Who's there?
Al.
Al who?
Al give you some Easter
candy if you ask nicely!

Knock knock.
Who's there?
Andrew.
Andrew who?
Andrew a picture of
the Easter bunny!

Knock knock.
Who's there?
Aaron.
Aaron who?
Aaron you glad it's Easter?

Knock knock.
Who's there?
Lena.
Lena who?
Lena little closer, I have an
Easter joke for you!

Knock knock.
Who's there?
Ivor.
Ivor who?
Ivor you give back my
Easter egg, or I tell Mom!

Knock knock.
Who's there?
Keanu.
Keanu who?
Keanu please share your
Easter eggs?

Knock knock.
Who's there?
Carmen.
Carmen who?
Are you Carmen over for Easter?

Knock knock.
Who's there?
Isaiah.
Isaiah who?
Isaiah nothing until you eat
all your Easter dinner too!

Knock knock.
Who's there?
Isma.
Isma who?
Where Isma
Easter bunny outfit?

Knock knock.
Who's there?
Pete.
Pete who?
Can we eat Pete-za
for Easter lunch?

Knock knock.
Who's there?
Ada.
Ada who?
Ada had too many
chocolate Easter eggs!

Knock knock.
Who's there?
Abbott.
Abbott who?
Abbott time for Easter dessert, isn't it?

Knock knock.
Who's there?
Alba.
Alba who?
Alba helping with the Easter decorations!

Knock knock.
Who's there?
Duncan.
Duncan who?
Duncan your chickens before
they've hatched!

Knock knock.
Who's there?
Alva.
Alva who?
Alva nother helping
of ice cream, please!

NAMES

Knock knock.
Who's there?
Bert.
Bert who?
Mom, the Easter
dinner is bert!

Knock knock.
Who's there?
Dee.
Dee who?
Dee-liscious Easter food
on the way!

Knock knock.
Who's there?
Grover.
Grover who?
Let's Grover there.
I see more eggs!

Knock knock.
Who's there?
Gino.
Gino who?
Gino an Easter
joke, too?

Knock knock.
Who's there?
Hammond.
Hammond who?
Hammond eggs
for Easter
breakfast, please!

KNOCK KNOCK JOKES FOR KIDS. EASTER EDITION

Knock knock.
Who's there?
Les.
Les who?
Les go to buy Easter candy!

Knock knock.
Who's there?
Sid.
Sid who?
Sid down at the Easter table.
It's dinnertime!

Knock knock.
Who's there?
Amos.
Amos who?
Amos Easter time again!

Knock knock.
Who's there?
Imogen.
Imogen who?
Imogen if you guessed
this Easter joke!

Knock knock.
Who's there?
Frank.
Frank who?
Frank you for coming to my
house for Easter!

NAMES

Knock knock.
Who's there?
Yetta.
Yetta who?
Yetta nother great Easter holiday is over!

Knock knock.
Who's there?
Goliath.
Golaith who?
Goliath down, you look eggs-hausted!

Knock knock.
Who's there?
Isaac.

Isaac who?
Isaac at telling good
Easter jokes!

Knock knock.
Who's there?
Alex.
Alex who?
Alex-plain later what stuffers
I got in my Easter basket!

Knock knock.
Who's there?
Amy.
Amy who?
Amy fraid I forgot to
bring your Easter gift!

KNOCK KNOCK JOKES FOR KIDS. EASTER EDITION

Knock knock.
Who's there?
Joe.
Joe who?
I like to tell Easter Joe-kes!

Knock knock.
Who's there?
Juno.
Juno who?
Juno where all the Easter
eggs are hiding?

Knock knock.
Who's there?
Will.
Will who?
Will you share your
Easter candy with me?

Knock knock.
Who's there?
Eudy.
Eudy who?
Eudy-serve an Easter
egg or two!

Knock knock.
Who's there?
Alfie.
Alfie who?
Alfie sick from eating too
many chocolate eggs!

NAMES

3

ANIMALS

Knock knock.
Who's there?
Bunny.
Bunny who?
Bunny, I'm home!

Knock knock.
Who's there?
Eezer.
Eezer who?
There's an Eezer bunny
in the yard!

Knock knock.
Who's there?
Iguana.
Iguana who?
Iguana eat some
Easter eggs!

Knock knock.
Who's there?
Hare.
Hare who?
There is chocolate in
your hare!

Knock knock.
Who's there?
Alpaca.
Alpaca who?
Alpaca the toys, you
pack-a the sweets!

Knock knock.
Who's there?
Who.
Who who?
I didn't know owls
like Easter!

Knock knock.
Who's there?
Some bunny.
Some bunny who?
Some-bunny ate all
the Easter eggs!

Knock knock.
Who's there?
Chicken.
Chicken who?
Chicken your basket to see
how many eggs ya got!

Knock knock.
Who's there?
Moose.
Moose who?
Moose you know all the
good Easter jokes?

Knock knock.
Who's there?
Honeybee.
Honeybee who?
Honeybee kind to
everyone during Easter!

ANIMALS

Knock knock.
Who's there?
Howl.
Howl who?
Howl I know when it is Easter?

Knock knock.
Who's there?
Lion.
Lion who?
I need to lion down after all this Easter food!

Knock knock.
Who's there?
Roach.
Roach who?
Roach a letter to the Easter Bunny today!

Knock knock.
Who's there?
Rhino.
Rhino who?
Rhino many funny Easter jokes!

Knock knock.
Who's there?
Herd.
Herd who?
Have you herd it's Easter?

Knock knock.
Who's there?
Viper.
Viper who?
Viper face, It's got chocolate all over it!

Knock knock.
Who's there?
Dragon.
Dragon who?
You are dragon your feet on this egg hunt!

Knock knock.
Who's there?
Rabbit.
Rabbit who?
Rabbit up. Mom says it's
time for Easter dinner.

Knock knock.
Who's there?
Herring.
Herring who?
I've been herring some
corny Easter jokes!

Knock knock.
Who's there?
Gopher.
Gopher who?
Wanna gopher an
Easter ice cream?

Knock knock.
Who's there?
Geese.
Geese who?
Geese where we are
going for Easter.

Knock knock.
Who's there?
Cod.
Cod who?
I cod lost on the
Easter Egg hunt!

Knock knock.
Who's there?
Fangs.
Fangs who?
Fangs for inviting
us for Easter!

Knock knock.
Who's there?
Kung fu.
Kung fu who?
Every bunny was
kung fu fighting!

Knock knock.
Who's there?
There's.
There's who?
There's no bunny like you!

Knock knock.
Who's there?
Hoppy.
Hoppy who?
Hoppy Easter Sunday!

Knock knock.
Who's there?
Hen.
Hen who?
I am very hen-gry!
When's Easter lunch?

Knock knock.
Who's there?
Bison.
Bison who?
Please bison cookies for Easter!

Knock knock.
Who's there?
Bach.
Bach who?
Bach, bach said the chicken!

Knock knock.
Who's there?
Owl.
Owl who?
Owl be seeing you
at Easter!

Knock knock.
Who's there?
Goat.
Goat who?
We need to goat
to the store
for some more
Easter eggs!

Knock knock.
Who's there?
A moose.
A moose who?
Aren't my Easter jokes
a-moosing you?

Knock knock.
Who's there?
Cat.
Cat who?
The cat is feline
fine this Easter!

Knock knock.
Who's there?
Peck.
Peck who?
This Easter lunch was
im-peck-able!

Knock knock.
Who's there?
Boar.
Boar who?
Hey! My Easter jokes are
not boar-ing!

Knock knock.
Who's there?
Fleas.
Fleas who?
Fleas, can you give me
some more of your
Easter Eggs?

KNOCK KNOCK JOKES FOR KIDS. EASTER EDITION

BODY

Knock knock.
Who's there?
Nose.
Nose who?
He nose where all the Easter eggs are hidden!

Knock knock.
Who's there?
Urine.
Urine who?
Urine trouble for eating
candy before Easter dinner!

Knock knock.
Who's there?
Mustache.
Mustache who?
I mustache you for an
Easter joke later!

Knock knock.
Who's there?
Ears.
Ears who?
Ears another Easter
knock-knock joke for you!

Knock knock.
Who's there?
Tooth.
Tooth who?
Will Easter lunch be
ready at tooth-30?

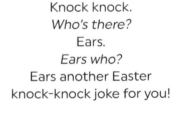

Knock knock.
Who's there?
Lung.
Lung who?
We be-lung together for Easter.

Knock knock.
Who's there?
B.
B who?
It's Easter. B-positive!

Knock knock.
Who's there?
Bad.
Bad who?
Bad Easter jokes
are how eye roll!

Knock knock.
Who's there?
Organ.
Organ who?
Will you help me
organ-ize the table
for Easter lunch?

BODY

Knock knock.
Who's there?
Etch.
Etch who?
Euuueeewww, next time use a tissue!

Knock knock.
Who's there?
Waist.
Waist who?
Wasn't this Easter joke a waist of your time?

Knock knock.
Who's there?
Belly.
Belly who?
I can belly stand all this amazing Easter food!

5

FOOD AND EASTER CELEBRATIONS

Knock knock.
Who's there?
Lettuce.
Lettuce who?
Lettuce enjoy Easter time with family!

Knock knock.
Who's there?
Butter.
Butter who?
You butter like my Easter jokes!

Knock knock.
Who's there?
Juicy.
Juicy who?
Juicy how many Easter eggs that kid got?

KNOCK KNOCK JOKES FOR KIDS. EASTER EDITION

Knock knock.
Who's there?
Orange.
Orange who?
Orange you glad we took part
in the Easter egg hunt?

Knock knock.
Who's there?
Chow.
Chow who?
Guess what? It is Easter
chow time!

Knock knock.
Who's there?
Peas.
Peas who?
Peas pass me
the chicken!

Knock knock.
Who's there?
Pudding.
Pudding who?
Pudding your shoes on is
necessary if we're going
Easter egg hunting!

FOOD AND EASTER CELEBRATIONS

Knock knock.
Who's there?
Cash.
Cash who?
No thanks, I would prefer peanuts for an Easter snack!

Knock knock.
Who's there?
Loaf.
Loaf who?
I loaf coloring in Easter pictures.

Knock knock.
Who's there?
Olive.
Olive who?
Olive Easter!

Knock knock.
Who's there?
Two knee.
Two knee who?
Mom is making two knee fish sandwiches for Easter lunch!

Knock knock.
Who's there?
Water.
Water who?
Water you doing for Easter?

Knock knock.
Who's there?
Turnip.
Turnip who?
When will everyone turnip
for Easter lunch?

Knock knock.
Who's there?
Quiche.
Quiche who?
Give grandma a hug and a
quiche for Easter.

Knock knock.
Who's there?
Cereal.
Cereal who?
Cereal pleasure to help you
set the Easter table!

Knock knock.
Who's there?
Carrot.
Carrot who?
I don't carrot all for vegetables.

Knock knock.
Who's there?
Donut
Donut who?
Donut disturb Dad, he's napping!

Knock knock.
Who's there?
Peas.
Peas who?
Easter should be a peas-ful time!

Knock knock.
Who's there?
Peeled.
Peeled who?
Keep your eyes peeled for
the Easter Bunny!

Knock knock.
Who's there?
Cabbage.
Cabbage who?
The cabbage won the Easter
race because he was a-head!

Knock knock.
Who's there?
Ketchup.
Ketchup who?
Mom invited her friend for
Easter dinner, and they had a
lot of ketchup-ping to do.

Knock knock.
Who's there?
Leek.
Leek who?
Leek over there, I see
more Easter eggs!

Knock knock.
Who's there?
Sultan.
Sultan who?
Remember to put sultan pepper
on the Easter table!

Knock knock.
Who's there?
Nacho.
Nacho who?
Stay away. These are nacho Easter eggs!

Knock knock.
Who's there?
Bean.
Bean who?
Bean a while since we saw you for Easter!

Knock knock.
Who's there?
Chick.
Chick who?
Chick-ken catch-a-tore
on the Easter menu!

Knock knock.
Who's there?
Eat.
Eat who?
Eat all your veggies or no
Easter pudding for you!

Knock knock.
Who's there?
Yam.
Yam who?
"I yam what I yam," said the
Easter sweet potato!

KNOCK KNOCK JOKES FOR KIDS. EASTER EDITION

Knock knock.
Who's there?
Taco.
Taco who?
Taco bout a good
Easter break!

Knock knock.
Who's there?
Dill.
Dill who?
You have to share
your Easter eggs, so
just dill with it!

Knock knock.
Who's there?
Bacon.
Bacon who?
It smells like you are bacon
some Easter biscuits. Yum!

Knock knock.
Who's there?
Calm.
Calm who?
Lettuce romaine calm!

Knock knock.
Who's there?
Gouda.
Gouda who?
We gouda get dressed
for Easter lunch now!

FOOD AND EASTER CELEBRATIONS

Knock knock.
Who's there?
Beef.
Beef who?
You need to wash your
hands beef-fore we eat!

Knock knock.
Who's there?
Kiwi.
Kiwi who?
Kiwi paint Easter eggs now?

Knock knock.
Who's there?
Mushroom.
Mushroom who?
There is not mushroom
around the Easter
dinner table!

Knock knock.
Who's there?
Wurst.
Wurst who?
Eating vegetables
is the wurst!

Knock knock.
Who's there?
Sea.
Sea who?
I sea so much candy and I
want to eat all of it!

Knock knock.
Who's there?
Brie.
Brie who?
I don't like to disa-Brie
with you at Easter!

Knock knock.
Who's there?
Dessert.
Dessert who?
You don't dessert another
slice of Easter pie!

Knock knock.
Who's there?
Feta.
Feta who?
Don't feta about your friends;
you can see them over
the Easter break!

FOOD AND EASTER CELEBRATIONS

Knock knock.
Who's there?
Latte.
Latte who?
I have a whole latte
love for my family!

Knock knock.
Who's there?
Cookie.
Cookie who?
That Easter cookie looks weir-dough!

Knock knock.
Who's there?
Mango.
Mango who?
My Easter jokes are mango-nificent!

Knock knock.
Who's there?
Dairy.
Dairy who?
Try and take all my
Easter candy, I
dairy you!

Knock knock.
Who's there?
Cake.
Cake who?
Mom's Easter cake is so pretty, I am in tiers!

Knock knock.
Who's there?
Choc.
Choc who?
A chocolate bunny! Choc it out!

Knock knock.
Who's there?
Bun.
Bun who?
Easter is all bun and dusted!

Knock knock
Who's there?
S'more.
S'more who?
S'more Easter
pudding, please!

Knock knock.
Who's there?
Pear.
Pear who?
This Easter was pear-fect!

6

EASTER EGG DECORATING

Knock knock.
Who's there?
Dyeing.
Dyeing *who?*
I am dyeing to know what we are doing for Easter!

Knock knock.
Who's there?
Dye.
Dye who?
Those Easter eggs
are to dye for!

Knock knock.
Who's there?
Stencil.
Stencil who?
Easter was brought to
a stencil in 2020!

Knock knock.
Who's there?
Arts.
Arts who?
This Easter drawing
is off the arts!

Knock knock.
Who's there?
Paint.
Paint who?
Are you feeling paint
of heart this Easter?

Knock knock.
Who's there?
Draw.
Draw who?
Who wins the Easter prize is the luck of the draw!

Knock knock.
Who's there?
Clay.
Clay who?
An apple a clay keeps
the doctor away!

Knock knock.
Who's there?
Caesars.
Ceasars who?
Please hand me
the Caesars.

Knock knock.
Who's there?
Drafts.
Drafts who?
I want to do some
Easter arts and drafts!

Knock knock.
Who's there?
Pink.
Pink who?
I pink we have decorated
enough eggs now!

Knock knock.
Who's there?
Tuba.
Tuba who?
Please can I have a tuba glue
for my Easter project?

Knock knock.
Who's there?
Broken.
Broken who?
This broken crayon is pointless!

EASTER FUN
AND
THINGS

Knock knock.
Who's there?
Barbie.
Barbie who?
We are having an
Easter Barbie-Q!

Knock knock.
Who's there?
Ken.
Ken who?
Ken we please hunt for
more Easter eggs?

Knock knock.
Who's there?
Leg.
Leg who?
Leg-OH! I just stepped
on an Easter toy!

Knock knock.
Who's there?
Lego.
Lego who?
Lego of me, and I will
give you an Easter egg!

Knock knock.
Who's there?
Re-tail.
Re-tail who?
We need some Easter basket
stuffers from the re-tail store!

Knock knock.
Who's there?
Disco.
Disco who?
The Easter playlist got
disco-nected!

Knock knock.
Who's there?
Voodoo.
Voodoo who?
Voodoo you think decorates
eggs the best?

Knock knock.
Who's there?
Needle.
Needle who?
I needle little help carrying
my Easter basket, please!

EASTER FUN AND THINGS

Knock knock.
Who's there?
Irish.
Irish who?
Irish you a happy
Easter holiday!

Knock knock.
Who's there?
Ya.
Ya who?
Ya who! Mom made my
favorite meal for Easter!

Knock knock.
Who's there?
Bed.
Bed who?
Bed you didn't see this
Easter joke coming!

Knock knock.
Who's there?
Razor.
Razor who?
Razor glasses for
an Easter toast!

Knock knock.
Who's there?
Leash.
Leash who?
Leash you can do is share
your Easter eggs!

Knock knock.
Who's there?
Police.
Police who?
Police may I have
some Easter candy?

Knock knock.
Who's there?
Closure.
Closure who?
Closure mouth when
eating Easter eggs!

Knock knock.
Who's there?
Comb.
Comb who?
Comb down and eat
your Easter eggs!

Knock knock.
Who's there?
Tank.
Tank who?
Tank you for all my
Easter treats!

Knock knock.
Who's there?
Cents.
Cents who?
This Easter joke makes
no cents at all!

EASTER FUN AND THINGS

Knock knock.
Who's there?
Iran.
Iran who?
Iran the fastest in the Easter race today!

Knock knock.
Who's there?
White.
White who?
See you Easter morning, white and early!

Knock knock.

Who's there?
Just.
Just who?
Just hanging with all
my family this Easter!

Knock knock.
Who's there?
Icy.
Icy who?
Icy many Easter eggs!

Knock knock.
Who's there?
Avenue.
Avenue who?
Avenue got any
Easter eggs left?

Knock knock.
Who's there?
Heaven.
Heaven who?
Heaven-t you heard enough
Easter jokes already today?

Knock knock.
Who's there?
Ho-ho.
Ho-ho who?
It's Easter, not Christmas!

Knock knock.
Who's there?
Sony.
Sony who?
No, it's not the Easter
Bunny. Sony me!

Knock knock.
Who's there?
Handsome.
Handsome who?
Handsome more Easter
candy to share?

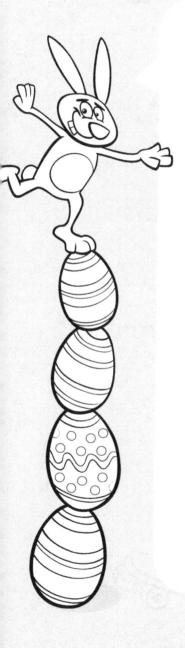

Knock knock.
Who's there?
Gray.
Gray who?
Gray the Easter force be with you!

Knock knock.
Who's there?
Plato.
Plato who?
Plato Easter cookies, please!

Knock knock.
Who's there?
Pen.
Pen who?
Count to pen, and my egg is done!

Knock knock.
Who's there?
Chalk.
Chalk who?
I don't want to spend
Easter in chalk-down!

Knock knock.
Who's there?
Watts.
Watts who?
Watts for Easter breakfast?
I am hungry!

Knock knock.
Who's there?
Easter-ly.
Easter-ly who?
The wind is blowing in an Easter-
ly direction this Easter!

Knock knock.
Who's there?
Best.
Best who?
Best you get up, or we will be
late for the Easter feast!

Knock knock.
Who's there?
Here.
Here who?
I am here to make you
laugh at Easter!

Knock knock.
Who's there?
Can.
Can who?
Can we go hunt for
Easter eggs now?

Knock knock.
Who's there?
Havana.
Havana who?
I'm Havana a great time
this Easter with you!

Knock knock.
Who's there?
Burglar.
Burglar who?
Can I have a ham-
burglar and chips for
Easter lunch, please?

Knock knock.
Who's there?
Witches.
Witches who?
Witches the way to the
Easter egg hunt?

Knock knock.
Who's there?
Screams.
Screams who?
I am bursting at the screams
from all these Easter jokes!

Knock knock.
Who's there?
Oil.
Oil who?
Oil in oil, it was a great Easter.

Knock knock.
Who's there?
Supplies.
Supplies who?
SUPPLIES! We came
to visit for Easter!

Knock knock.
Who's there?
Chemistry.
Chemistry who?
Ha! I was hoping to get
a reaction from you!

EASTER FUN AND THINGS

Who's there?
Yoke.
Yoke who?
It was just a little Easter yoke!

Knock knock.
Who's there?
Zero.
Zero who?
Thanks for nothing!

Knock knock.
Who's there?
Week.
Week who?
Seven days without my Easter
jokes will leave you week!

Knock knock.
Who's there?
Ready.
Ready who?
Are you ready for
more Easter jokes?

Knock knock.
Who's there?
Hop.
Hop who?
It's Easter. Let's hop to it!

8

SPRING

Knock knock.
Who's there?
Great.
Great who?
Ears to a great Easter break!

Knock knock.
Who's there?
Hatch.
Hatch who?
Are you sneezing from the spring flowers?

Knock knock.
Who's there?
Spring.
Spring who?
Easter puts a spring in my step!

Knock knock.
Who's there?
Egg.
Egg who?
I am egg-stremely glad to
see the spring flowers!

KNOCK KNOCK JOKES FOR KIDS. EASTER EDITION

Knock knock.
Who's there?
Orchid.
Orchid who?
Don't you understand my
spring jokes? Well, this
is an orchid situation!

Knock knock.
Who's there?
Pansies.
Pansies who?
I want to see the chimp-
pansies at the zoo!

Knock knock.
Who's there?
Floret.
Floret who?
Go on! Floret and
drive faster!

Knock knock.
Who's there?
Pollen.
Pollen who?
I am pollen your leg with
all these spring jokes!

Knock knock.
Who's there?
Grounded.
Grounded who?
Mom says you are
grounded for life!

Knock knock.
Who's there?
Grow.
Grow who?
All dressed up and nowhere
to grow this Spring break!

Knock knock.
Who's there?
Forest.
Forest who?
Run, Forest, run!

Knock knock.
Who's there?
Wooden.
Wooden who?
Our car wooden start
this morning!

Knock knock.
Who's there?
Re-leaf.
Re-leaf who?
What a re-leaf
winter is over!

Knock knock.
Who's there?
Urchin.
Urchin who?
I am urchin from the grass!

Knock knock.
Who's there?
Bud.
Bud who?
Last bud not least!

Knock knock.
Who's there?
Seed.
Seed who?
Did you seed that?

Knock knock.
Who's there?
Wind.
Wind who?
This wind today simply blows!

Knock knock.
Who's there?
Tulips.
Tulips who?
Tulips are needed for kissing!
Knock knock.

Who's there?
Hive.
Hive who?
My brother is on his best
bee-hive-ior today!

Knock knock.
Who's there?
Shady.
Shady who?
I don't trust those trees.
They look kinda shady!

Knock knock.
Who's there?
Mist.
Mist who?
I sure mist you a lot!

Knock knock.
Who's there?
Plants.
Plants who?
I laughed so hard, I almost wet my plants!

Knock knock.
Who's there?
Dew.
Dew who?
How dew you dew?

Knock knock.
Who's there?
Sunny.
Sunny who?
Sunny body out there?

Knock knock.
Who's there?
Gnome.
Gnome who?
No gnome-school today, it's Spring break!

Knock knock.
Who's there?
Sand.
Sand who?
The sand is wet because of the sea peed!

Knock knock.
Who's there?
Sea-sun.
Sea-sun who?
It's Spring sea-sun!

Knock knock.
Who's there?
Canoe.
Canoe who?
Canoe come over to play
during Easter break?

SPRING

BEFORE YOU GO

Did you have fun with those sometimes corny, sometimes punny Easter knock-knock jokes?

Now that you have gotten the hang of knock-knock jokes, spend some time thinking up some of your own! Create your own jokes using family traditions or fun things you like to do with your friends.

For Easter, you can create knock-knock jokes about the Easter Bunny, Easter baskets, Easter traditions, the fun you can have at Easter celebrations, the food you eat for Easter, and the candy you get in your Easter baskets.

Once you think up your own knock-knock jokes, you can play the game anywhere! It is a great game to play on long road trips, at school or even when you are waiting in line at the grocery store.

Have fun coming up with your own jokes and endless giggles!

WRITE YOUR OWN JOKES!

Have fun coming up with your own jokes and endless giggles!

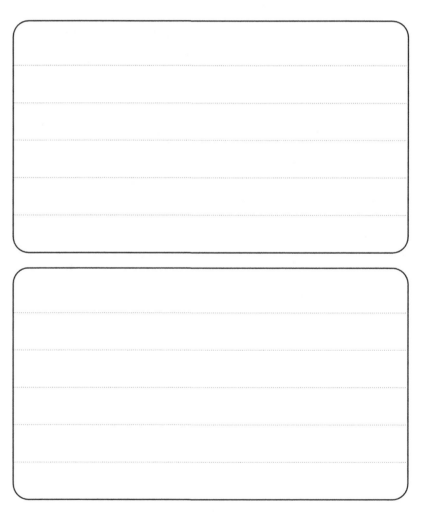

WRITE YOUR OWN JOKES!

KNOCK KNOCK JOKES FOR KIDS. EASTER EDITION

WRITE YOUR OWN JOKES!

WRITE YOUR OWN JOKES!

KNOCK KNOCK JOKES FOR KIDS. EASTER EDITION

WRITE YOUR OWN JOKES!

KNOCK KNOCK JOKES FOR KIDS. EASTER EDITION

WRITE YOUR OWN JOKES!

KNOCK KNOCK JOKES FOR KIDS. EASTER EDITION

KNOCK KNOCK JOKES FOR KIDS. EASTER EDITION

KNOCK KNOCK JOKES FOR KIDS. EASTER EDITION

KNOCK KNOCK JOKES FOR KIDS. EASTER EDITION

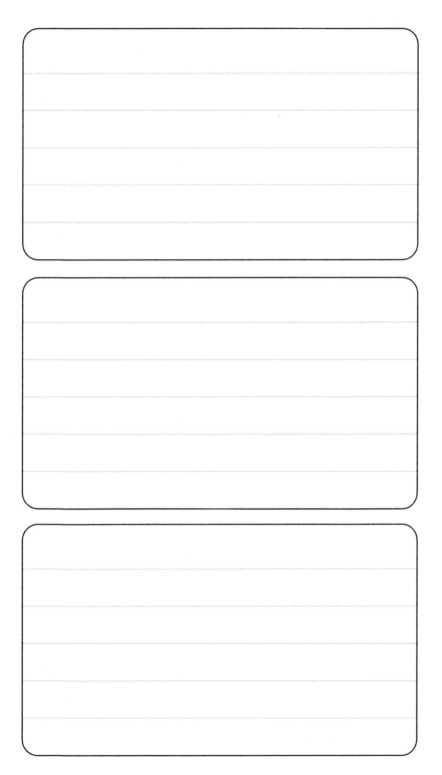

WRITE YOUR OWN JOKES!

KNOCK KNOCK JOKES FOR KIDS. EASTER EDITION

WRITE YOUR OWN JOKES!

WRITE YOUR OWN JOKES!

COLLECT THEM ALL!

Would You
Rather for Kids
Easter Edition

Easter
Joke Book
for Kids

Easter Knock
Knock Joke
Book for Kids

www.riddlesandgiggles.com

REFERENCES

Easter Knock Knock Jokes For Kids. The Simple Parent. (2020, April 2). The Simple Parent. https://thesimpleparent.com/easter-knock-knock-jokes-for-kids/

Knock Knock Animal Jokes - Knock Knock Jokes. (n.d.). Www.jokes4us.com. http://www.jokes4us.com/knockknockjokes/knockknockanimaljokes.html

Larkin, B. (2019, October 28). 100 Knock Knock Jokes Guaranteed to Crack You Up. Best Life; Best Life. https://bestlifeonline.com/knock-knock-jokes/

Matej. (2020, October 18). 175 Best Egg Puns That Are Simply Egg-ceptional. Czech the World. https://czechtheworld.com/egg-puns/

Parade. (2019, November 5). 101 Knock Knock Jokes — Best Knock Knock Jokes for Kids. Parade; Parade. https://parade.com/944054/parade/Knock knock.-jokes/

Walsh, G. (2020, April 29). Best Knock knock. jokes for kids. GoodtoKnow. https://www.goodto.com/family/children/best-Knock knock.-jokes-for-kids-538236

Wynne, M. (2020, September 3). 65 Best Plant Jokes That You'll Be Very Frond Of by Kidadl. Kidadl.com. https://kidadl.com/articles/best-plant-jokes-that-youll-be-very-frond-of

Made in United States
North Haven, CT
14 March 2023

34081555R00059